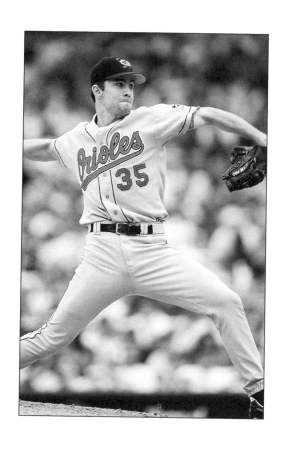

BALTIMORE

RICHARD RAMBECK

THE HISTORY OF TH

ORIOLES

CREATIVE EDUCATION

Published by Creative Education
123 South Broad Street, Mankato, Minnesota 56001
Creative Education is an imprint of The Creative Company

Designed by Rita Marshall
Editorial assistance by Rosemary Wallner and John Nichols

Photos by: Allsport Photography, Archive Photos, Focus on Sports,
Fotosport, SportsChrome.

Library of Congress Cataloging-in-Publication Data

Rambeck, Richard.
The History of the Baltimore Orioles / by Richard Rambeck.
p. cm. — (Baseball)
Summary: Highlights the key personalities and memorable games in the
history of the team that changed its name to the Orioles when it moved
to Baltimore from St. Louis in 1954.
ISBN: 0-88682-899-6

1. Baltimore Orioles (Baseball team)—History—Juvenile literature.
[1. Baltimore Orioles (Baseball team)—History. 2. Baseball—History.]
I. Title. II. Series: Baseball (Mankato, Minn.)

GV875.B2R355 1999
796.357'64'097526—dc21   97-6343

First edition

9 8 7 6 5 4 3 2 1

Much of the economic activity in the state of Maryland centers on its largest city, Baltimore, which is one of the busiest ports in the United States. Located on beautiful Chesapeake Bay, Baltimore is one of America's oldest and most culturally rich communities.

Part of Baltimore's rich history is a major league baseball team that, since it moved to the Maryland city in 1954, has had one of the finest records in the game. The team, named the Orioles after Maryland's state bird, has given the Baltimore fans much to cheer about during the last four decades,

Hard-hitting catcher Gus Triandos.

including three World Series championships and six American League pennants.

To draw fans to see the St. Louis Browns, owner Bill Veeck inserted 3-foot-7 Eddie Gaedel into the lineup.

The Baltimore franchise actually began in St. Louis. Known as the Browns, the St. Louis club was one of the least successful teams in the American League. It joined the league in 1902 but didn't win a pennant until 1944. Led by Vern Stephens, who topped the American League in runs batted in with 109, the team posted an 89–65 record. In the World Series, the Browns faced their crosstown rivals, the St. Louis Cardinals. The Cards had claimed their third consecutive National League title with an incredible 105–49 record, but the Browns weren't intimidated. St. Louis' "other" team won two of the first three games of the series. The Cardinals, however, rallied to take the last three outings, winning the World Series four games to two.

A year after playing in the World Series, the Browns fell to last place. By 1951, when Bill Veeck bought the team, the Browns were among the worst clubs in the majors. Veeck decided the team's future was not in St. Louis; he looked around and found a group in Baltimore interested in buying the Browns. The group, led by Baltimore attorney Clarence W. Miles, purchased the club for $2.4 million. The Browns moved to Maryland in 1954 and changed their name to the Orioles.

The Baltimore fans, who had long supported minor-league teams, immediately fell in love with their new club. More than one million fans saw the Orioles play in 1954, when they finished seventh in the eight-team American League. The fan support enabled the club to make a profit of nearly one million dollars. But the team still wasn't successful. Clearly, some of that money had to be used to develop

The incomparable Cal Ripken Jr.

young talent. Lindsay Deal, a member of the Orioles' front office, already had his eye on a prospect, a third baseman named Brooks Robinson.

BROOKS ROBINSON BUILDS DEFENSE

In the team's second season in Baltimore, Paul Richards became the new manager of the Orioles.

On February 13, 1955, Lindsay Deal wrote to former teammate Paul Richards (who would soon become the Orioles' general manager). "Dear Paul, I am writing you in regard to a kid named Brooks Robinson. I think he measures up to having a chance in major league baseball. I think he is a natural third baseman, although he has been playing both second and third. This boy is the best prospect I've seen since Billy Goodman came to Atlanta to play when I was playing there."

Deal proved to have a good eye for talent. The Orioles signed Robinson, and seven months after Deal wrote to Richards, Robinson became the first prospect to make the team after it left St. Louis. Robinson brought two outstanding attributes to the Orioles: his great fielding and his great attitude. His two basic beliefs were "All's well that ends well," and "Most things do end well."

In 1959 Robinson's baseball career nearly came to an abrupt end. Chasing a foul ball into a dugout, Robinson caught his arm on a steel hook, cutting several nerves and tendons. While doctors put 22 stitches in his arm, he joked with the nurses—even though he knew he might never bend his elbow again. Six weeks later, Robinson fought his way back into the lineup.

Robinson also had to fight through occasional hitting

slumps early in his career. One season, team officials decided to send Robinson down to the minor leagues to regain his batting stroke, but a group of Baltimore pitchers went to general manager Richards and begged him to keep Robinson on the team. "They didn't care if he never got a hit," Richards said. The pitchers wanted him in the game for his fielding. Eventually, Robinson's hitting would improve with experience. In 1964 he hit .317, led the American League in runs batted in with 118, and won the AL MVP award. Despite Robinson's heroics, the Orioles were not pennant contenders—that is, not until 1966.

Big James Gentile slammed 46 homers, including five grand slams, for the Orioles.

FRANK ROBINSON PROVES TO BE A TRIPLE THREAT

The Orioles made a bold trade before the 1966 season began, sending pitcher Milt Pappas and two journeyman players to the Cincinnati Reds for right fielder Frank Robinson. Robinson, the 1961 National League MVP, had been a star for years in the NL, but Reds general manager Bill DeWitt believed Robinson's best days were behind him. Although Robinson was only 30 years old, DeWitt claimed that he was "an old 30" and made the move. He couldn't have been more wrong. Baltimore manager Hank Bauer put the two Robinsons (Frank and Brooks) back-to-back in the batting order, and it paid off.

In Baltimore's first four games of 1966, each Robinson had three home runs; in addition, Brooks had eight RBIs and Frank had six. Later that year, Frank Robinson dazzled Orioles fans by clouting a 540-foot home run that sailed over the bleacher wall in Baltimore's Memorial Stadium; he was

Switch-hitting first baseman Eddie Murray.

Powerful catcher Chris Hoiles.

Shortstop Luis Aparicio's 57 stolen bases during the season set an Orioles team record.

the first player ever to do that. "He really creamed it," Brooks Robinson said. "He's a tremendous guy to be playing with and to hit behind. He gets on base so often, and he can steal and set up a run for us."

Frank Robinson was a bold hitter who crowded the plate and often led the major leagues in number of times hit by pitches. "Nobody has ever had more guts at the plate than Frank," said Earl Weaver, who would become the Orioles' manager in 1968. "He actually curled his upper body and head over the plate and dared pitchers to hit him."

The player who the Reds thought was washed up had a remarkable year in 1966. He wound up leading the American League in homers (49), runs batted in (122), and batting average (.316), making him the first American Leaguer since Mickey Mantle in 1956 to claim the Triple Crown. Named the American League Most Valuable Player, he became the only man ever to win the MVP award in both leagues. Robinson also led the Orioles to their first-ever AL pennant.

In the World Series against the Los Angeles Dodgers, both Robinsons hit home runs to spark Baltimore to a 5–2 opening game upset. The favored Dodgers never recovered, and the Orioles stormed to a four-games-to-none sweep. As good as the Robinsons were in the series, though, the Baltimore pitching was even better. Dave McNally, Wally Bunker, and a 20-year-old phenom named Jim Palmer shut down Los Angeles, not allowing a single run the last three games of the series. "To do that to a ballclub as good as the Dodgers is almost unthinkable," exclaimed a joyous Brooks Robinson after the last game. "I'm just glad I was here to see it, otherwise I wouldn't have believed it."

Unfortunately, the Orioles were unable to maintain their championship ways. Hank Bauer was fired as manager in the middle of the 1968 season and replaced by Earl Weaver, who had coached Baltimore's top minor-league team. Weaver inherited a team of players who disliked each other almost as much as they disliked Bauer. When he took over, Weaver told the players that his door was always open and that they should feel free to take their complaints to him. The players heard Weaver's speech and then left. "The only player who walked into my office after the meeting was Frank Robinson," Weaver said. "The best player in all of baseball said, 'If there's anything I can do to help, let me know.' I appreciated that."

It also gave Weaver the opportunity to assume command. He had Robinson, a player all of the Orioles looked up to and listened to, behind him. Suddenly, the Orioles started to play much better, going 48–34 in the games Weaver managed at the end of the 1968 season. The ingredients were in place for another pennant run in 1969.

Before the season, the Orioles, who already had two fine starting pitchers in Dave McNally and Jim Palmer, added another standout starter, Mike Cuellar, in a trade with the Houston Astros. In his first season with the club, Cuellar won 23 games and shared the 1969 Cy Young Award with the Detroit Tigers' Denny McClain. The Orioles, fueled by their stellar pitching, dominated the race in the American League East Division. (The league was divided into two divisions before the 1969 season.) Baltimore won

1 9 6 6

Dave McNally led the Orioles in wins (22), innings pitched (273.0), and ERA (1.95).

13

The towering Boog Powell terrorized opposing pitchers by slamming 37 homers and driving in 121 runs.

109 games, the most victories by a major-league team in eight years.

The Orioles had great hitting from Frank Robinson, first baseman Boog Powell, and outfielders Paul Blair and Don Buford. The team also had great fielders: Brooks Robinson, shortstop Mark Belanger, second baseman Davey Johnson, and Blair. Led by these stars, Baltimore swept AL West winner Minnesota in the American League Championship Series three games to zero.

In the World Series, however, the Orioles ran into the amazing New York Mets. Not long before, the Mets had been one of the worst teams in baseball. But after Cuellar pitched Baltimore to a 4–1 victory in game one, the Mets rallied behind pitchers Tom Seaver and Jerry Koosman to take the series four games to one.

In 1970 the Orioles again romped to the AL East title, this time winning 108 games. The Orioles then beat Minnesota in the league championship series to earn the right to play the "Big Red Machine" of Cincinnati in the World Series. Many experts picked the Reds, but the Orioles, and Brooks Robinson in particular, were determined not to let this series slip away.

It didn't start well for Robinson and the Orioles, though. The first time a ball was hit to Robinson in the series, he made a bad throw that turned into a two-base error. But he vowed not to let the mistake get to him, and it didn't. Robinson proceeded to put on a fielding performance that is unmatched in World Series history. Several times he dove to snag sure base hits and turn them into outs. "I've seen all the greatest third basemen over the last 50 years—'Home Run' Baker, 'Pie' Traynor, Eddie Mathews," said former New York

The 1969 Orioles were above all competition.

1 9 7 0

World Series MVP Brooks Robinson earned the nickname "Hoover" (after the vacuum cleaner) for his strong defense.

Yankees manager Casey Stengel. "I don't say he [Robinson] is any better than they were, but he compares with them. Don't hit it to that fellow." Led by Robinson, who was named MVP, the Orioles won the series four games to one.

A year later, in 1971, the Orioles won another American League East title and then defeated the Oakland Athletics to earn a spot in their third-straight World Series. Among American League teams, only the New York Yankees, Philadelphia Athletics (who eventually became the Oakland Athletics), and Detroit Tigers had played in three consecutive World Series. The Orioles, however, were not able to capture the '71 fall classic. After triumphing in the first two games against the Pittsburgh Pirates, Baltimore then dropped three in a row and eventually lost, four games to three.

Despite that World Series disappointment, the Orioles remained one of the top teams in the American League. They won the AL East in 1973 and 1974, but lost both years to the eventual world champion Oakland A's in the league championship series. By 1977, however, the Orioles' stars had gotten old and, in some cases, had retired. Brooks Robinson ended his magnificent career after 23 seasons and a record 16 Gold Glove awards for fielding excellence. Frank Robinson had left to take a job as the manager of the Cleveland Indians, becoming the first black manager in major-league history.

Earl Weaver wondered how he would replace Frank Robinson. "He had great, great baseball instincts and tremendous physical attributes that allowed him to do everything right on a ballfield," Weaver said. "It's sad to say, but Baltimore will never have another Frank Robinson." That may be true, but when Robinson left the Orioles, another leader emerged. This time it was a pitcher: Jim Palmer.

PALMER MAKES A PITCH AT LEADERSHIP

Jim Palmer was one of the most dominant major-league pitchers during the 1970s. His devastating high fastball, pinpoint control, and keen understanding of how to pitch made him a star of Hall of Fame quality. In fact, Palmer, who won three Cy Young Awards as the American League's top pitcher in 1973, 1975, and 1976, was elected to the Hall of Fame in 1990. "Palmer is a great pitcher, certainly one of the all-time greats," said Earl Weaver. "I can't count all the big games he has won for us. . . . He has risen to the occasion as much as any pitcher in baseball."

Jim Palmer was awarded his second Gold Glove, sharing the honor with teammate Mark Belanger.

It was unusual for Weaver to praise Palmer, as the two often fought through the newspapers and on television. Palmer, who suffered nagging injuries, would say he was unable to pitch, and Weaver would say the whole thing was in Palmer's head. They may have fought, but the Orioles' star pitcher was a role model for the younger players. "He's like having another pitching coach around," said Baltimore pitching coach Ray Miller. "When the other players see a guy like Palmer working hard and taking care of himself, it does more good than anything you can tell them."

Despite Palmer's leadership, the Orioles, who won five AL East titles in six years from 1969 to 1974, went without a division championship for the next five seasons. But the team was building a stable of new stars, including young pitchers Mike Flanagan and Scott McGregor and first

1977 Rookie of the Year Eddie Murray (pages 18-19).

Right-hander Steve Stone recorded 25 victories and earned the AL Cy Young Award.

baseman Eddie Murray, who in 1977 was named Rookie of the Year in the American League. In 1979 Flanagan, who won the American League Cy Young Award, and Palmer pitched the Orioles to an AL East Division title. Baltimore then beat the California Angels in the league championship series. For the first time in eight years, the Orioles had made it to the World Series. They had the same opponent, the Pittsburgh Pirates, as they had had eight years before. Unfortunately for the Orioles, the result was also the same. The Pirates beat Baltimore four games to three for the World Series title.

The 1979 AL pennant was to be the last the Orioles won under fiery Earl Weaver, whose frustrations increased when Baltimore finished second in the division from 1980 through 1982. The Milwaukee Brewers defeated the Orioles on the final day of the 1982 regular season to claim the AL East title. Weaver then announced his retirement. When the 1983 season began, the Orioles had a new manager for the first time in 15 years: Joe Altobelli. They also had an emerging new star: shortstop Cal Ripken Jr.

RIPKEN—A CHIP OFF THE OLD BLOCK

Cal Ripken Jr. played his first season for the Orioles in 1982, but he'd been around the club all his life. His father, Cal Ripken Sr., had been a coach since before his son was born. Growing up, the younger Cal would often ride with his father to Orioles practices. "When dad first asked if I wanted to go to the ballpark with him, I went because I could be with him alone on the drive there and back," Ripken said. "Eventually I began to enjoy baseball." He also began to learn baseball. "I'd go ask someone, say [Baltimore third baseman] Doug DeCinces, about how to do a certain thing. Then when he told me, I'd go ask my dad if what he told me was right. My dad was always the final authority, and if he told me the guy gave me correct information, I knew I could go back to him."

When Cal Ripken Jr. joined the Orioles, it became impossible to move him out of the starting lineup. In fact, he never missed an inning, let alone a game. "A lot of people go to work every day and it doesn't make headlines," he said. "This is my job, and I love doing it." The hardworking Ripken missed only three games in 1982, none after May 29, and for his productive efforts (.264 average, 28 homers, and 93 RBIs) he was named the American League Rookie of the Year. In 1983 Ripken had an even better year, winning the AL Most Valuable Player Award. During the season he amassed 221 hits, scored 121 runs, and hit 47 doubles. Ripken, Eddie Murray, and designated hitter Ken Singleton powered the Orioles' offense, and rookie pitcher Mike Boddicker filled in admirably for the injured Jim Palmer and threw five shutouts.

Baltimore rolled to the AL East title and then defeated Chicago for the American League pennant. In the World Series, the Orioles lost the first game to the Philadelphia Phillies and then won four straight to claim their first World Series title since 1970.

The Orioles had reached the top again, but they would soon fall to the bottom. Joe Altobelli was fired in 1985 and replaced by Earl Weaver, who quit for good after the 1987

1 9 8 2

After 14 years as the Baltimore club's manager, Earl Weaver retired; he returned three years later.

21

Orioles ace Jim Palmer.

season. In 1988 the Orioles started the season by losing their first 21 games, a major-league record for futility. Out of the misery though, the Orioles were able to give many of their younger players a lot of major-league experience. This seasoning helped the next year. The Orioles were suddenly transformed from an awful team to an awesome team in 1989. Closer Gregg Olson led the way, posting 27 saves and capturing the AL Rookie of the Year award.

The Orioles, who won only 54 games in 1988, posted an 87–75 record in 1989, finishing a close second in the AL East to the Toronto Blue Jays. Baltimore actually led the division for most of the season before being overtaken by Toronto in September. In 1990, though, the team fell behind Boston and Toronto early in the season and never caught up. The season's biggest highlight was the 95-game errorless streak by Cal Ripken Jr., a major-league record for shortstops. "Sometimes I think the guy is a robot," joked Minnesota Twins manager Tom Kelly. "He doesn't make mistakes, and he plays every single day."

1 9 9 1

Led by the powerful Ben McDonald, the Baltimore pitching staff became one of baseball's finest.

"IRON" CAL MAKES HISTORY

In 1992 the Orioles' franchise began a new chapter in its history when the team moved from old Memorial Stadium to beautiful new Oriole Park at Camden Yards. The classical design of the new stadium made it an instant landmark in Baltimore. Legions of fans came to see what would become the model for the modern baseball facility.

The Orioles provided their fans with a steady, consistent winner from 1992 to 1994, but unfortunately, there would be

Chris Hoiles had 82 RBIs—an Orioles catchers' record—and led the team in average (.310) and homers (29).

no division titles to show for it. In 1995 the team took a step backward, finishing 71–73, but on the night of September 6, Orioles fans, and baseball fans around the world, were treated to a very special moment. That night, Cal Ripken Jr. started at shortstop for the Orioles against the California Angels. Ordinarily it was not a major event, but on this night the ordinary had become the extraordinary.

Ripken was playing in his 2,131st game, breaking the major-league record for consecutive games played set in 1939 by New York Yankees legend Lou "Iron Horse" Gehrig. The amazing Ripken had not missed a game in nearly 14 seasons. With the game stopped for the ceremony, Ripken gave a speech crediting family and friends, but afterward, in an incredibly moving gesture, "Iron" Cal jogged around the stadium shaking hands with the wildly cheering fans. "It's the least I could do," said Ripken. "Those fans have been with me every step of the way."

Ripken did not stop the streak there. He continued to play every day for the Orioles, and at the end of the 1997 season, the mark stood at an incredible 2,478 games. Ripken also holds the record for most career home runs by a shortstop with 345, passing Chicago Cubs great Ernie Banks in 1993.

In 1996 the Orioles and Ripken returned to their usual winning ways. The team's biggest weapon was a lineup stocked with home-run power: center fielder Brady Anderson led the way with 50; first baseman Rafael Palmeiro clouted 39; designated-hitter Bobby Bonilla smacked 28; Ripken powered 26; catcher Chris Hoiles blasted 25; second baseman Roberto Alomar hit 22; and third baseman B. J. Surhoff swatted 21 round-trippers.

By the end of the 1996 season, the Orioles had battered American League pitching for 257 home runs, shattering the old major-league record of 240, set by the 1961 New York Yankees. The homers also paved the way for 88 victories, good enough to earn Baltimore a spot in the playoffs.

In the postseason, the Orioles stormed past the favored Cleveland Indians in the divisional series three games to one. The upset victory earned the Orioles a chance to play their longtime rivals the New York Yankees for the AL championship. Baltimore fans expected the home-run barrage to continue against the Yankees, but first baseman Rafael Palmeiro issued a disclaimer. "We don't really have a plan," he said. "If the home runs come, then they come."

The fans' expectations were high, however, as the Orioles battled the Yankees. But an unexpected event derailed the team's momentum. In game one, in the bottom of the eighth inning, Yankees shortstop Derek Jeter hit a deep fly ball. Right fielder Tony Tarasco ran under the ball at the fence and held up his glove. Just as the ball came down, however, a 12-year-old fan sitting in the first row reached his glove over Tarasco's glove and knocked the ball into the stands.

The umpire ruled Jeter's hit a home run. Despite protests from players, fans, and coaches that the youngster had interfered with Tarasco, the umpire's ruling stood. The Yankees tied the game and went on to win in the 11th inning, 4–3. The Yankees won the AL championship, four games to one.

The loss was devastating, but the team still had much to celebrate. The Orioles franchise had returned to prominence, and expectations were high for 1997.

1 9 9 4

Pitcher Mike Mussina led the Baltimore club in wins (16), innings pitched (176.1), and ERA (3.06).

The energetic Brady Anderson (pages 26-27).

1 9 9 5

Scott Erickson came to Baltimore in a trade with the Minnesota Twins on July 7, then went 9–4 the rest of the way.

Before the 1997 season, the Orioles' management and coaching staff took a long, hard look at their team of power hitters. They knew that if they wanted to get to the playoffs again, they needed to improve their pitching and defense. With those goals in mind, the club signed left-handed pitcher Jimmy Key and shortstop Mike Bordick.

When fans heard that a new shortstop had been signed, many wondered how Cal Ripken would handle a move to third base. Ever the team player, Ripken agreed to the move. "I do what's in the best interests of the ballclub," he said.

Manager Davey Johnson's team came together quickly. Brady Anderson was back in center field and star right-handed pitcher Mike Mussina looked sharper than ever. One new addition was pitching coach Ray Miller, who had worked with Earl Weaver 12 years before.

The revamped Orioles still packed plenty of offensive punch, but the new additions gave Baltimore a more versatile and effective club. From the first day of the 1997 season until the last, the Orioles kept a stranglehold on first place in the AL East. Baltimore captured the division title with a 98-64 record, becoming only the sixth team in major-league history to spend every day of the season in first place.

In the first round of the playoffs, the Orioles beat the Seattle Mariners to advance to the American League Championship Series against the Cleveland Indians. In a hard-fought series, the Indians ended the Orioles' World Series hopes, defeating them four games to two. "We've been close the last two years," explained a determined Brady

The powerful Rafael Palmeiro.

Gold Glove second baseman Roberto Alomar.

Outstanding defensive shortstop Mike Bordick.   31

Eric Davis was anticipating a great year after hitting .304 with eight home runs the previous season.

Anderson. "We've taken our lumps, but I believe we can win this thing."

The Orioles still have the weapons to contend. With a batting order featuring Anderson, Roberto Alomar, Rafael Palmeiro, and Ripken, they have the dangerous combination of speed and power. The Orioles' run-scoring machine should continue to terrorize the league for years to come.

On the pitching side, the Orioles possess a starting rotation that can measure up with the best in baseball. Mussina, Scott Erickson, crafty veteran Jimmy Key, and Scott Kamieniecki combined for 57 wins in 1997. In the bullpen, blazing-fast left-hander Armando Benitez is set to become the late-inning stopper. Benitez's fastball is routinely clocked at more than 100 mph, and in 1997, opposing batsmen hit for a sickly .191 average against him. "Armando is just one nasty guy to face," said teammate Palmeiro. "Sometimes it's easier to hear his pitches than see them."

The Orioles also have added new leadership. Pitching coach Ray Miller took over as manager following Johnson's resignation after the 1997 season. "I've been with this organization a long time, and I've been with other clubs too," stated Miller. "The Baltimore Orioles are all about championship baseball, and I have every intention of keeping that tradition alive and well."

With Ripken, Mussina, Anderson, and Palmeiro leading the way, the Orioles are poised to take the next big step toward their fourth World Series championship.